not a guide to

Exeter

Suze Gardner

To Glen
for helping me in and out of
so many memorable scrapes

First published 2013

The History Press
The Mill, Brimscombe Port
Stroud, Gloucestershire, GL5 2QG
www.thehistorypress.co.uk

British Library Cataloguing in Publication Data.
A catalogue record for this book is available from the British Library.

ISBN 978 0 7524 7967 5

Typesetting and origination by The History Press
Printed in Great Britain

Coat of Arms

The motto *Semper Fidelis* (ever faithful) was suggested by Queen Elizabeth I in thanks for Exeter's support against the Spanish Armada.

The castle is Rougemont, dating from 1068. The gatehouse still stands today.

Holy Roman Emperor, the powerful Richard I, Duke of Cornwall, is represented by the lion. The orb which the lion holds denotes Richard's 'Royal' status.

Exeter's important maritime trade is commemorated by the two white horses which symbolise the River Exe.

Contents

Acknowledgements

Thanks to Seal for his encouragement; to Nina and my colleagues at Exeter City Council; Exeter's Red Coat Guides; David Cornforth at Exeter Memories; Roger at the Devon and Exeter Institution; Exeter Cathedral; the *Express & Echo*; Exeter City Football Club; and Exeter Chiefs Rugby Club.

Welcome to

EXETER

the Regional Capital

Pronunciation and Definition

Prounounced EK-si-ter

The Roman name for Exeter was Isca Dumnoniorum, which meant 'the town of the Dumnonii'. The Romans built the settlement here around AD 50. The Dumnonii were an Iron Age tribe who inhabited much of the West Country, including parts of what is now Exeter, at the time of the Roman invasion.

Grid Reference

Exeter Cathedral – SX 92057 92510

Latitude: 50.722157

Longitude: -3.5305519

Street Names

Exeter's street names often reflect its 2,000-year-old history. They give clues to its former importance as a centre of religious learning and celebrate the trade and industry which once flourished in the city.

Blackboy Road: The nickname of Charles II because of his dark colouring.

Buddle Lane: From an Old English word 'bothl' which means 'dwelling'.

Friernhay Street: Meaning 'friars enclosure'. Grey Friars lived in the area in the late 1200s.

Guinea Street: Derives from the old word 'gennel', meaning 'narrow road'.

Heavitree Road: A Saxon word; Heavitree means 'the head tree' – one used as a gallows.

Mincinglake Road: From an ancient name for nuns – 'Moenchin' – and a stream near a nunnery.

Parliament Street: One of the narrowest streets in the world. Urban myth suggests that it referred to the capability of eighteenth-century government!

Rack Street: 'Rack' refers to frames to dry the woollen cloth for which Exeter was famed.

Sidwell Street: From the mythical St Sidwella, an early Christian killed by her stepmother.

Waterbeer Street: From the 1300s. It was the street of water bearers who collected river water to sell.

Widgery Road: Named after F.J. Widgery, a famous landscape painter and mayor of Exeter, in 1903.

Areas of Exeter

Alphington: Though part of Exeter today, Alphington retains its former village feel and has countryside close at hand.

Cowick: The name 'Cowick' is Saxon. A priory was located in Cowick until 1538. Many other old buildings were cleared in the 1970s, though historically interesting ones remain.

Duryard: The University of Exeter is located here. Duryard Valley Park is a green area, once part of a Royal hunting ground.

Exwick: Exwick's proximity to the river meant that it had mills from the Saxon era onwards.

Heavitree: Formerly the first village on the road to London from Exeter, Heavitree is east of the city centre.

Mincinglake: Mincinglake includes parts of Stoke Hill and Beacon Heath. The valley park forms part of Exeter's picturesque Green Circle.

Newtown: Though damaged in the bombing of 1942, there is a vibrant community spirit in Newtown, which is home to popular Belmont Park.

Pennsylvania: On raised land north of the city centre, Pennsylvania is popular with students. It was named after the US state in 1820.

Pinhoe: Formerly a separate village, Pinhoe became part of Exeter in the 1960s. Today it forms part of the route of famous Great West Run.

Polsloe: A Saxon, 'Poll' owned the land here; 'Polsloe' means 'Poll's marsh'. A priory, St Katherine's, was founded here in 1159 and dissolved during the reign of Henry VIII.

St David's: A thousand years ago there were farms here. Exeter's expansion incorporated St David's in the nineteenth century. The area is home to the university's Streatham Campus.

St James: Situated in the north of the city and home to Exeter City Football Club. St James has buildings of all ages from the 1800s onwards.

St Leonard's: Leafy St Leonard's has attractive Georgian and Victorian houses. The parish was once the smallest in Devon but has expanded over time.

St Loye's: The Ludwell Valley Park gives St Loye's some picturesque views close by. The reputedly haunted remains of the thirteenth-century St Loye's chapel are worth a visit.

St Thomas: The Exe Bridge connects St Thomas, which is west of the River Exe, to the centre of Exeter.

Topsham: Famous for its architecture and maritime history. Actress Vivian Leigh married a local solicitor here in 1932. Topsham Museum holds Leigh memorabilia.

Whipton: The area now known as Whipton has nothing to do with whip manufacturing! The name derives from the fact that the land was once owned by a Saxon called 'Wippa'.

Distance From ...

Place	Miles	Km
Ayers Rock, Australia	9,475	15,250
Brussels, Belgium	345	555
Centre of the Earth	3,975	6,397
Death Valley, USA	5,189	8,351
Eiffel Tower, Paris	289	468
Frankfurt, Germany	538	867
Guernsey, UK	98	157
Hong Kong, China	6,126	9,873
Isle of Man, UK	246	397
Jerusalem, Israel	2,359	3,798
The Kremlin, Russia	1,710	2,752
London Eye, UK	157	253
The Moon (average distance)	238,857	384,403
The North Pole	2,714	4,368
Osaka, Japan	6,031	9,707
The Panama Canal, Republic of Panama	5,128	8,254
Queenstown, New Zealand	11,905	19,160
Reykjavik, Iceland	1,142	1,839
The Sun	93mil	149mil
The Taj Mahal, India	4,432	7,133
Ural Mountains, Russia	2,519	4,053
Vatican City	974	1,566
Washington DC, USA	3,541	5,699
Xanthi, Greece	1,502	2,422
Yellowstone National Park, USA	4,541	7,309
Zurich, Switzerland	689	1,109

Strange but True

In December 1961 a wooden house over 450 years old was moved, intact, because it was in the way of a new bypass. After being clad in a protective wooden frame, the building was hoisted onto wheels and moved uphill about 200ft from its original location on Frog Street to its present position on West Street. Today the picturesque Tudor building is home to a bridal shop.

In 1829, the list of tolls on goods unloaded from ships at Exeter Quay included: bones and hooves at 2s per barrel; hair at 2s 6d for 40ft; woad at 1s 6d per barrel; mops at 1d per dozen; a four-wheeled coach incurred 7s 6d; fresh fish, up to six dozen, free; manure at 10d per ton; and chimney pots at 1d each.

In an upstairs room at Exeter Custom House, original eighteenth-century wallpaper can still be seen in a cupboard. Protected from the light for many years, it is still possible to make out rows of blue flowers on a cream background.

And One That Isn't True!
Exeter's Underground Passages are not haunted by 'Albert', a man on a penny-farthing bicycle. The story was dreamed up by an overenthusiastic tour guide who was entertaining children on a Halloween trip in the 1990s.

Twinned Towns

Rennes, France
With a population of 200,000, Rennes is the capital of the region of Brittany. The earliest architectural remains in Rennes are the third-century fortifications, but there are many beautiful medieval and eighteenth-century buildings. Particularly eye-catching are the colourful traditional houses. Rennes was twinned with Exeter in 1956.

Bad Homburg, Germany
A spa town famous for its medicinal mineral waters and Homburg hats. British holidaymakers have enjoyed relaxing in Bad Homburg since the Victorian era when the town became popular with Britain's monarchy. It is one of the wealthiest towns in Germany due to its location near the beautiful Taunus Mountains. Bad Homburg was twinned with Exeter in 1965.

Terracina, Italy
Situated just 56km south of Rome, ancient Terracina is a stunning mixture of beautiful beaches and well-preserved Roman and Byzantine remains. The modern town, with 70,000 inhabitants, is built sympathetically to fit in with its ancient buildings of which the locals are very proud. Terracina was twinned with Exeter in 1988.

Yaroslavl, Russia
In the centre of the Russian Plain, Yaroslavl has a population of 630,000 and is the largest city in the region. It is known as one of Russia's most beautiful cities because of the stunning sixteenth- and seventeenth-century architecture and its location at the confluence of the Volga and Kotorosl rivers. Yaroslavl was twinned with Exeter in 1989.

Other Exeters

Exeter, Tulare County, California, USA

Exeter, Monroe County, Michigan, USA

Exeter, Fillmore County, Nebraska, USA

Exeter, Penobscot County, Maine, USA

Exeter, Washington County, Rhode Island, USA

Exeter, Scott County, Illinois, USA

Exeter, New London County, Connecticut, USA

Exeter, Luzerne County, Pennsylvania, USA

Exeter, Otsego County, New York, USA

Exeter, Barry County, Missouri, USA

Exeter Green County, Wisconsin, USA

Exeter, Rockingham County, New Hampshire, USA

Exeter, Ontario, Huron County, Canada

Exeter, LeFevre, South Australia, Australia

Exeter, Wingecarribee Shire, New South Wales, Australia

Exeter, Tasmania, Australia

Historical Timeline

The stone city wall is constructed.

Leofric is made the first Bishop of Exeter.

Many residents are killed by the Black Death.

An Iron Age settlement is located in what is now Southernhay, Exeter.

The Danes capture the city.

After sixty years the Norman cathedral is finished.

200 BC   200   876   1050   1180   1348

AD 40-55   670   1001   1068   1284   1369

Roman forces build a fortress and bathhouse near today's cathedral.

King Sweyn of the Vikings attacks Exeter.

Trade is affected by a weir built over the Exe by Countess de Fortibus.

William the Conqueror lays siege to Exeter after the city rebels.

Exeter is known as 'Isca Chester'.

A new cathedral reaches completion.

John Trew builds the Exeter canal allowing maritime trade to expand.

Over 400 people die of cholera. Many victims were interred at Bury Meadow.

Exeter airport is opened.

Exeter's famous Custom House is built on the quay.

Theatre Royal fire kills 186. It was Britain's worst theatre fire and forced safety changes.

The new Princesshay shopping centre is completed.

1564   1680   1832   1885   1938   2007

1642   1770   1868   1902   1942   2011

The Civil War begins. Exeter is besieged by each side in turn.

The Royal Albert Memorial Museum & Art Gallery opens.

The Blitz kills over 265 people, and destroys large areas of Exeter.

England's first inn to be called a 'hotel' is built. It is now the Royal Clarence.

The city's first moving picture show is seen by Exeter dignitaries.

The Royal Albert Memorial Museum & Art Gallery reopens following extensive refurbishment.

Freak Weather

1880

A prolonged spell of unusually cold weather caused parts of the River Exe to freeze over. Enormous ice chunks which had broken away were seen floating under the Exe Bridge, making the river unnavigable for several days.

1891

Between 8 and 12 March, severe blizzard conditions caused a train to become stuck in a snowdrift at Powderham near Exeter. After spending the night crowded round a makeshift fire, passengers were rescued by a train from Exeter, which had been fitted with a snow plough.

1960

On 27 October, more than half of Exeter's annual rainfall came at once, causing flooding in many areas of the city. Over 1,000 properties were inundated with up to 6ft of water. Further flooding on 3 December led to the construction of extensive flood defences.

2012

Between 23 and 28 April, torrential rain caused both the River Exe and River Creedy to burst their respective banks. The water became a vast fast-flowing torrent near Cowley Bridge. Nearby fields were turned into a large lake. It took five days for the flood water to subside.

A Day in the Life of the City

08.30 – Morning prayers echo through Exeter's beautiful Cathedral Church of Saint Peter.

09.00 – Early lectures at the University of Exeter begin.

10.00 – The newly refurbished award-winning Royal Albert Memorial Museum & Art Gallery opens its doors to visitors.

11.00 – Exeter's famous and knowledgeable Red Coat Guides start their varied free walking tour programme.

12.00 – Afternoon visits to the fascinating and unusual medieval Underground Passages begin.

16.00 – Luxury afternoon tea is underway at Michael Caines Champagne Bar, ABode Hotel, overlooking the picturesque cathedral.

17.00 – The last visitors leave the Royal Albert Memorial Museum & Art Gallery.

17.30 – The controversial and inconvenient closing time of Stagecoach Exeter's Enquiries Office.

19.30 – Curtain up on performances at The New Theatre, Exeter

23.00 – Cool live music at Mama Stone's venue is in full swing.

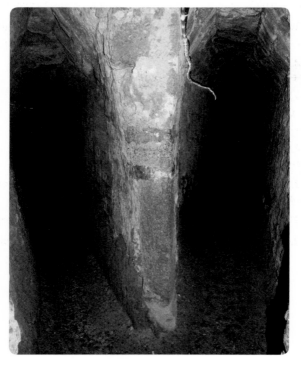

How Many Times a Year ...

The *Express & Echo* is published: 52

(The paper was daily until 2012)

The Mayor of Exeter attends Civic Ceremonies: 20

(Other events attended by the busy mayor run into hundreds)

Visitors explore the Underground Passages: 19,000

Shops in the city centre open late for Christmas shopping: 5

(Thursdays in November and December)

Visitors go into the cathedral: 110,000

Exeter City FC play at home: 26

Exeter's intrepid Red Coat Guides run tours, rain or shine: 363

(There are no tours on Christmas Day or Boxing Day)

Demographics

Total population: 111,080

Aged under 16: 16,741

Aged 16–64: 77,094

Aged 64 and over: 17,245

Female population: 57,136

Male population: 53,944

Marital Status
Males who have never married: 28,268

Males married: 19,703

Males separated: 844

Males divorced: 3,757

Males widowed: 1,376

Females who have never married: 25,329

Females married: 19,408

Females separated: 1,167

Females divorced: 5,125

Females widowed: 6,101

Ethnicity

White British: 105,231

White Irish: 671

White Other: 2,562

White/Black Caribbean: 178

White/Black African: 111

White/Other: 626

Asian–Indian: 280

Asian–Pakistani: 71

Asian–Bangladeshi: 140

Asian/Other: 235

Black Caribbean: 52

Black African: 140

Black/Other: 27

Chinese: 742

Strange Statistics

The number of Bishops of Exeter (1046 to the present): 70

The cost of the Royal Albert Memorial Museum & Art Gallery's renovation and expansion completed in 2011: £24 million

The number of cars in Exeter in 1912: 225

The number of cinemas in Exeter in the 1930s (there are 3 today): 10

Cost of the Heavitree Arch, a controversial sculpture erected at Gordon's Place in 2008: £70,000

The number of times the Rolling Stones have played in Exeter since 1964: 4

Exeter's population in 1931 (in 2011 it was 111,078): 66,029

Estimated number of cholera deaths in the 1832 outbreak: 400

Average house price in Exeter in 2010: £208,400

Number of military hospitals set up in Exeter during the First World War: 5

First year trams arrived in Exeter (the last one was in 1931): 1905

The year the city got its first computer: 1962

The year the first internet café in Exeter opened: 1996

Literary Quotations

'… Exeter, a city famous for two things, which we
seldom find unite in the same town, (viz.) that 'tis
full of gentry, and good company, and yet full of trade
and manufactures also; the serge market held here
every week is very well worth a strangers seeing …
The people assur'd me that at this market is generally
sold from 60 to 70 to 80, and sometimes a hundred
thousand pounds value in serges in a week.'

Daniel Defoe – *A Tour Through the
Whole Island of Great Britain* (1727)

'The disease had raged in various parts of England … yet
on its bursting forth within the city, its existence was
denied … then, as the disease progressed, the people
became appalled and, repenting, appealed by prayer, to
the Great Disposer of all events, to stay the pestilence. '

Dr Thomas Shapter –
History of Cholera in Exeter in 1832 (1849)

REPORT

on the

STATE OF EXETER.

By THOMAS SHAPTER, M.D.,

'I cannot go without recording my obligations to everyone in the house; if it is your fate to fall sick at an inn, pray heaven it may be the New London, Exeter'.

Diary of Robert Louis Stevenson (1885)

'Wherever Jude heard of free-stone work to be done, thither he went, choosing by preference places remote from his old haunts … sometimes as far down as Exonbury.'

Thomas Hardy – Jude the Obscure (1895) *Exonbury was a fictionalised term for Exeter

'You come to me not alone, but as agent of my friend Peter Hawkins of Exeter, to tell me all about my new estate.'

Count Dracula to Jonathan Harker in Bram Stoker's Dracula (1897)

'The Misses Durnford … moved to Exeter, and took lodgings in St. Sidwell's parish … they dressed in strange fashions. In their early days they made themselves conspicuous by introducing the bloomer arrangement in the nether latitude. This, as you may well suppose, was regarded as a scandal'.

Revd Sabine Baring Gould – Devonshire Characters and Strange Events (1908)

What the Famous Have Said About Exeter

Quotes from the *Express & Echo:*

'Hello you wonderful people of Exeter. It's great to be here in this beautiful city. I love Exeter!'

Michael Jackson, 2002

'Exeter is a fantastic city and it is a huge privilege to represent the people here.'

Ben Bradshaw, MP, 2010

'It has been absolutely fantastic … You just need to see and smell the local food … This is a great showcase for the South West and for Exeter.'

Top chef Michael Caines, 2011

'We did this out of respect. He (Michael Jackson) put Exeter City on the international map.'

Uri Gellar, after his friend Michael Jackson was made an honorary director of Exeter City FC, 2012

Famous For

Princess Henrietta Anne Stuart (1644–1670) was the youngest child of King Charles I. She was born at Bedford House in Exeter during the Civil War. Her father visited Bedford House – the only time he saw Henrietta.

J.K. Rowling (1965–) the *Harry Potter* author went to the University of Exeter where she began making notes for her future novels. Diagon Alley which features in the *Harry Potter* series is based on Exeter's Gandy Street.

Sir Francis Drake (1540–1596) is most famous for his role in defeating the Spanish Armada. He is said to have planned the campaign in Mol's Coffee House on Cathedral Close in Exeter. The nearby Ship Inn was Drake's favourite hostelry.

Tommy Cooper (1922–1984), renowned comedian and magician, was brought up in Exeter and went to Mount Radford School in the city. His first comic performance was at the age of sixteen.

Infamous For

The last executions for witchcraft in England took place in Exeter in 1682 when Temperance Lloyd, Suzanna Edwards and Mary Trembles were found guilty of the 'crime'. Today a plaque commemorating the unfortunate women can be seen on the wall of Exeter's Rougemont Castle. Recent research however suggests that Temperance, the last to be hanged, may well have been guilty of the multiple murders with which she was charged.

The worst theatre fire in England was at the Theatre Royal on Exeter's Longbrook Street which burned down in 1887 killing 186 people. Most of them were trapped due to inadequate safety exits. This was the second Theatre Royal in Exeter to be demolished by fire. In spite of this, safety had not improved.

Northcott Theatre Parking – the university campus location of Exeter's Northcott Theatre has always been controversial. In 2009 the theatre car park was closed for a teaching centre to be built on the land. Theatregoers have a 10-minute walk to the main car park, which shows no consideration for the disabled. The shuttle bus service between the two is inadequate, particularly when there are simultaneous events in the University Great Hall.

Drunken behaviour in the city centre over the past few years has led to increased concerns about the late-night antics of some young people. Fore Street, which has a number of pubs and clubs, has been highlighted by police as one of the worst areas in the city for drink-fuelled anti-social crimes. Unsurprisingly, most such crimes take place between 11 p.m. and 2 a.m. when revellers are back on the street. There is a significant police presence at that time.

THE DEVON WITCHES
IN MEMORY OF
Temperance Lloyd
Susannah Edwards
Mary Trembles
OF BIDEFORD DIED 1682
Alice Molland
DIED 1685
THE LAST PEOPLE IN ENGLAND
TO BE EXECUTED FOR WITCHCRAFT
TRIED HERE & HANGED AT HEAVITREE
In the hope of an end to persecution & intolerance

DEVON & CORNWALL
CONSTABULARY

Heavitree Road
Police Station
Exeter

Making the Headlines

2010–2011

An extensive Roman armoury and supply base was unearthed at the site of the former St Loye's campus. Significant finds included an early wooden writing tablet, the remains of leather shoes and a first century AD antefix – an ornamental roof-edging tile. The antefix is complete and features a human face.

November, 2010

John Lewis, one of Britain's leading retailers, took the lease on the former Debenhams department store building on Sidwell Street. This had been empty since the company moved into the new Princesshay shopping centre in 2007. City councillors welcomed the news that 180 new jobs would be created.

December, 2011

After four years and a multi-million pound refurbishment, Exeter's Royal Albert Memorial Museum & Art Gallery on Queen Street reopened with record visitor figures of over 3,500 in the first two days. Many items previously unseen by the public can be viewed along with new state-of-the-art interactive displays in the new extension to the rear.

Letters to the Press

Some serious subjects have traditionally been debated by the readers of the *Express & Echo*. Their letters, emails and later responses are often comical, sometimes ironic, occasionally extreme and always entertaining.

(These reader's letters and emails do not necessarily reflect the views of the *Express & Echo*.)

House Prices

The eternal subject of high house prices was addressed on 2 June 2011. A letter complained that everyone in the housing market, from buyers and sellers to estate agents, building societies, banks and financial advisors, all had their own agendas and that so-called experts deliberately set out to show the whole process in a bleak way to unsettle the populace.

Pension Woes

Another popular topic is the fairness or otherwise of the pensions system. On 25 June 2011 one reader commented about an acquaintance who, after working all his life and paying taxes and national insurance, decided to retire to the tropics. Unfortunately, the retiree then found that his UK pension, so carefully saved for, was frozen from the day he left Britain. The outraged reader stated that the situation was very wrong.

Occupy Exeter Protesters

A lively debate took place on 15 December 2011 when one reader wrote to criticise the anti-capitalists who had taken up residence in tents outside the cathedral in an attempt to make their point. In the writer's opinion something needed to be done to remove the protesters who were just messing about drinking and being a nuisance. It was their opinion that they should get jobs instead of complaining, or at least attempt to work out a valid alternative to the capitalism they despised.

Too Many Cars

Traffic problems were addressed on 10 June 2012 in the following (hopefully) ironic vein. A reader suggested ways to combat increased traffic congestion in Topsham. Much of this, the writer claimed, was down to cars of little value, driven by poor residents from less salubrious areas of the city, who, in fact, could not really afford trips out anyway. Perhaps, the writer suggested, right of way could be decided upon the value of vehicles and that non-residents should be made to wear bright armbands while in Topsham!

Rebellious Exeter

September, 2010

A day of protests against the repeal of the ban on hunting with dogs took place in Exeter and elsewhere in Devon. Protesters feared that a free vote in the House of Commons would see the ban overturned in spite of the fact that over 75 per cent of the population wanted it to remain. Animal Rights representatives accused pro-hunt Devon MPs of blatantly disregarding the majority of their constituents.

March, 2011

Around 5,000 government workers and their supporters held a peaceful march to protest against the government's proposed cuts in public sector pensions. Beginning at Exeter Cathedral, the chanting marchers, waving union banners, made their way to St James's football ground. Local union officials described the march as being part of the biggest countrywide day of demonstrations in a generation.

January, 2012

Cathedral officials urged the removal of the anti-capitalist 'Occupy Exeter' group who had been camped on Cathedral Green since November in protest against corporate greed. Anti-social behaviour from some of the group and inaccurate statements on the 'Occupy' Facebook page, led the previously sympathetic clergy to take a firmer stand.

Buildings and Architecture

Most Beautiful Old Building – Mol's Coffee House

Mol's is one of the most photographed buildings in Exeter. The windows contain over 130 tiny glass panes, and coupled with the timber frame they give the building a typically Tudor appearance – a date panel on the front says 1596. Mol's could be quite a lot older and was originally used to house priests. A number of legends have attached themselves to the building – the most famous of which being the claim that Francis Drake used the first floor as a headquarters when planning the defeat of the Spanish Armada in 1688. Its name may derive from Mary 'Mol' Wildy who ran a coffee shop there in the 1720s.

Most Beautiful Modern Structure – Miller's Crossing Bridge

This wonderful bridge shows how well old and new can blend if done sympathetically. Opened in 2002, Miller's Crossing foot and cycle bridge crosses the Exe near the eye-catching Blackaller Weir, on the section from Bonhay Road to Exwick Playing Fields. The 55m-long bridge is a cable structure. The ultra-modern A-frame support masts are held in place by two 6m mill stones which reflect the fact that there were once a number of mills in the area. The bridge is very popular with walkers, cyclists and sightseers.

Old and New – Princesshay Shopping Centre

Then

The first Princesshay shopping precinct replaced Georgian Bedford Circus and its surrounding area which was destroyed in the German bombing raid of 4 May 1942. Princesshay's claim to fame was that it was the first purpose-built pedestrian shopping area in England. Commencement of the development was marked by a commemorative phoenix plaque symbolising the rebirth of Exeter. This was unveiled by Princess Elizabeth (now the Queen) in 1949. Princesshay was completed in the early 1950s.

Now

After investment totalling £200 million and designs by internationally important architects, the new Princesshay shopping centre opened in 2007. The development is home to many popular high-street stores and restaurants, as well as stylish residential apartments. Though popular with most residents and visitors, inevitably the new Princesshay has its detractors. Most of these maintain that there are not enough individual local retailers and that lower-priced shops are under-represented.

Biggest Eyesore

Exeter Bus Station

Opened in 1964, the station is typical of the ugly concrete and brick designs of the time. The building is purely functional, with no consideration for aesthetic form. If the functionality of the place actually worked, that would be something in its favour. Unfortunately, it fails in this aspect too. The front of the building is open on three sides and acts like a wind tunnel which allows rain to be driven in. Recent plans for redevelopment have, so far, come to nothing.

Most Striking Architectural Feature

The Orangery, Imperial Hotel, New North Road

The Grade II listed Imperial was built in 1810 and was a private house until 1923. Today, the Imperial is owned by J D Wetherspoon. The huge barrel-vaulted Orangery was added around 1898 by keen gardener Dr William Hebden, who owned the building at that time. The Orangery, which draws visitors from miles around, features a beautiful semi-circular glass and iron window made in segments, representing an orange. This was based on one of engineer Isambard Kingdom Brunel's designs.

Most Interesting Monuments

The Clock Tower, Queen Street
and New North Road Junction

The Miles Memorial Drinking Fountain, to give this grand monument its original name, and gladden the heart of many an animal lover, was built in 1897 by the widow of William Miles, a wealthy local philanthropist and horse lover. The clock tower features red sandstone and incorporates horse troughs for the benefit of working horses.

The Deer Hunter

This statue is a striking bronze figure of a crouching hunter with his dog in classical style. The Deer Hunter is an 1886 work by Exeter sculptor Edward Bowring Stephens who was a Fellow of the Royal Academy. Stephens spent several years studying classical art in Italy. The statue stands impressively at the entrance of Northernhay Gardens.

Museums

The Royal Albert Memorial Museum & Art Gallery

After its recent multi-million pound refurbishment the RAMM, as the museum is popularly known, has become Exeter's flagship heritage venue, recently winning the Museum of the Year Award.

New and exciting hands-on activities and display areas with much more space allow more of RAMM's wonderful artefacts to be displayed and enjoyed. These include:

Local interest artefacts

Local and international History and Archaeology

World Cultures

Fine and Decorative Art

Costumes

Zoology and Botany

And old favourites like Gerald the Giraffe

Other must-see Museums and Heritage Sites in Exeter include:

The Bill Douglas Centre for the History of Cinema and Popular Culture

The Guildhall

Quay House Visitor Centre

St Nicholas Priory

Tuckers Hall

The Underground Passages

21 The Mint

Parks

First planted in the 1600s, Northernhay Gardens is the oldest and most central of Exeter's parks and is located just off the High Street. As well as its stunning plant displays and world-class sculptures, Northernhay Gardens is bordered on one side by Exeter's famous Roman wall. An archway leads into the adjacent Rougemont Gardens. From here Rougemont Castle gatehouse can be seen. Dating from 1068, this is the oldest of its kind in England. Other beautiful Exeter parks include:

Belle Isle Park

Belmont Park

Bull Meadow Park

Bury Meadow Park

Heavitree Pleasure Grounds

Pinces Gardens

St Thomas Pleasure Grounds

Southernhay Gardens

Green Spaces

The Green Circle
A trail around Exeter and its outskirts. Walkers experience the Roman wall, picturesque valleys, the River Exe and many historic villages. The route is 12 miles long, but its five sections can be walked separately.

Haldon Forest Park
An attractive area near the city for walkers, cyclists and horse riders. Quiet butterfly and nature trails contrast with the zany adventure area of zip-lines and rope bridges.

Southernhay Gardens
Once a private area for the Georgian townhouses which run on either side, today Southernhay Gardens are open to the public. Beautiful trees, carefully tended flowerbeds and benches provide a lovely space to relax in the centre of the city.

Local Flora and Fauna

The River Exe

An astonishing variety of bird life can be seen at Exeter Quay in the heart of the city. As well as the beautiful resident swans with their appealing cygnets, the area plays host to ducks, geese and a very active flock of starlings. Seabirds – waders and cormorants – have also been known to venture up the estuary to the quay.

Lucombe Oak

This extraordinary oak doesn't shed its leaves. It was first cross-bred from Turkey and Cork Oaks in 1762 by William Lucombe of Exeter. Fine examples can be seen at Southernhay Gardens and County Hall.

The Veitch Family

For over 170 years, until 1969, this family of botanists and gardeners ran a business in Exeter. They introduced over 1,000 varieties of exotic plants into England from all over the world. The Veitch Heritage Garden is in Southernhay.

Home-grown Businesses

Butts Ferry (established 1640s)
An unusual and popular feature of the River Exe, Butt's Ferry is a hand-operated cable ferry located at the quay. Passengers are carried in the aluminium vessel across the 46m wide river for the princely sum of 20p each way.

Garton & King (established 1661)
The business was started by John Atken on Fore Street and was a well-known ironmongery and forge. Today Garton King specialise in the supply and installation of AGA and Rayburn stoves and other appliances.

William Pollard & Co. (established 1781)
Pollard's is one of the oldest printers in Britain. Today it is a multi-million pound operation. Among its services are: publishing, branding, graphic design, marketing, stationery and web design.

Thomas Moore (established 1907)
Gentlemens' outfitter Thomas Moore was killed in action during the First World War. From the 1960s, the company began selling women and children's clothing and household items. Thomas Moore's toy department is the largest in the city centre.

Endicott's (established 1937)

Endicott's Military Surplus store grew due to the amount of stock available after the Second World War. Their expert knowledge has allowed them to cater to trends for military style clothing, offered at greatly reduced prices. Endicott's has remained a friendly, yet knowledgeable, family firm for over seventy years.

Dart's Farm (shop established 1970s)

Dart's Farm has expanded into a major shopping experience and it has won numerous awards. Locally produced foods and drinks are sold by experts, and independent traders sell many other products. Visitors can enjoy the summer Maize Maze and Animal Corner.

Exeter Quay Antique Centre (established on site in 1986)

Located in a former customs shed and fish warehouse, the centre has many separate traders all under one roof. They specialise in books, jewellery, toys, postcards, glass, pottery, tools, records and other items. The friendly traders welcome questions and offer expert advice.

Political Figures

Alured de Porta (?–1285)

De Porta was the only English mayor ever to be hanged. In 1283, he was implicated in the cathedral precinct murder of Walter Lechlade, an unpopular cathedral official. King Edward I came to Exeter to resolve the case. De Porta's execution took place on Boxing Day 1285. Gates were later added to the cathedral precinct for extra security. They were removed because of traffic hold-ups in the nineteenth century.

Frederick Widgery (1861–1942)

After studying at the Exeter School of Art and in London, Widgery went on to become a successful and prolific painter of West Country landscapes and seascapes. His work is admired by experts and amateurs alike for its composition and use of light. He returned to Exeter and set up a studio in the city. Becoming active in local politics, Widgery was elected mayor in 1903.

Gwyneth Dunwoody (1930–2008)

Labour MP for Exeter from 1966 to 1970, Dunwoody was England's longest-serving female MP and the only women ever to hold the position in Exeter. Both her grandmothers were suffragettes and like them she was known for her determination and forthright opinions. Dunwoody was notorious for her refusal to toe the party line and was unafraid of the trouble this got her into. Her daughter Tamsin is also an MP.

Ben Bradshaw

A former journalist at the *Express & Echo* newspaper, Ben Bradshaw has been the Labour MP for Exeter since 1997. He has held a number of high-profile positions in the Labour party, including Deputy Leader of the Commons, Minister for Health, and Culture Secretary. His campaign against the Japanese whaling industry and concern for the environment won him an animal welfare award. Ben was one of the first MPs to declare that he was gay.

Scientific Discoveries

Eleanor Coade (1733–1821)
Born in Exeter, she invented Coade Stone, a hard-wearing ceramic material which does not deteriorate in bad conditions. Coade Stone was incorporated into many famous landmarks in Britain, including Buckingham Palace. In Exeter, examples of Coade Stone can be seen at the cathedral and on buildings in Southernhay and Fore Street in Heavitree.

Charles Babbage (1791–1871)
Babbage went to school in Exeter. After observing the movements of cogs and gears in manufacturing machinery he invented the 'Difference Engine' and the 'Analytical Engine', the forerunners of today's modern computers. Today he is known as 'The Father of Computing'.

Dr Thomas Shapter (1809–1902)
Shapter was a young doctor in Exeter when a serious epidemic of cholera broke out in 1832. At the time the cause of the disease (infected drinking water) was not understood. In 1849, Shapter wrote *The History of the Cholera in Exeter* which was the most complete study of an epidemic and its progress written up to that time.

Isambard Kingdom Brunel (1806–1859)
In the 1830s Isambard Kingdom Brunel became the Chief Engineer of the Great Western Railway, which ran from London to Exeter. The line incorporated many of Brunel's innovative developments in tunnel design.

Local Characters in Unusual Occupations

Jon Freeman: The Bard of Exeter

After successfully working as a performance poet for many years, Jon became Exeter's Bard in January, beating seven other contestants to win the 'Bardic Chair'. He has since appeared on BBC Radio Devon, won poetry competitions and had some of his poetry published. Jon is the host of a monthly storytelling club at the City Gate Hotel and also runs 'Taking the Mic' at the Phoenix Art Centre.

Phil King Mace Sergeant

Exeter has had Mace Sergeants since the thirteenth century. Since 2009, the Senior Mace Sergeant and Mayoral Support Officer has been Phil King, an experienced ex-soldier. As well as officiating at civic functions wearing traditional robes of office, Phil's role includes: administrative support for the Lord Mayor; overseeing Civic ceremonies; and keeping a very complicated diary up to date. Phil says that in his job it is useful to be able to smile calmly at all times.

Crimes, Court Cases and Mysteries

'Good' John Barnes

Barnes was the landlord of the Black Horse in the 1670s. Although a tearaway in his youth, Barnes mended his ways when he met his religious wife. Sadly his reform didn't last because of money worries and he was caught thieving. During a prison break, in which Barnes refused to take part, the jailer's young son was killed. Though witnesses insisted that Barnes was not involved, he was hanged for it in 1678.

John Babbacombe Lee: 'The Man They Couldn't Hang'

In 1884, twenty-year-old Lee was found guilty of murdering his employer and was sentenced to hang. He continually claimed his innocence. On the gallows in Exeter prison, the drop lever failed to operate on three separate occasions. Throughout the procedure Lee remained perfectly calm. His sentence was commuted to twenty-two years imprisonment.

Giraffe Café Bomb

On 22 May 2008, a Muslim convert, Nicky Reilly, aged twenty-two, attempted to detonate a suicide bomb in the Giraffe Café in the city centre. It was lunchtime and the café and nearby streets were very busy, but fortunately the bomb failed to go off properly. At his trial, Reilly was found to have fallen under the influence of Muslim extremists. He was jailed for eighteen years.

The Santa Burglars

Criminals dubbed 'The Santa Burglars' raided dozens of Exeter homes in the run up to Christmas 2009. Ignoring expensive household items, the thieves targeted gift-wrapped presents amounting to thousands of pounds. Families were left very upset after the raids. A group of youths were later arrested for the crimes.

Ghosts

The Old Royal Devon and Exeter Hospital, Southernhay
The shadowy figure of a nurse has been seen at the windows of the now-derelict building. Locals believe her to be the ghost of a malevolent nurse from the Victorian period who predicted the deaths of patients by arranging their flowers into the shape of a cross.

Pedestrian Tunnel, Summer Lane
Loud banging noises, accompanied by groaning and screaming as if there is a fight going on, have been heard coming from the tunnel. When locals investigate there is nothing there, though the smell of blood has been reported.

Old Courts, Exeter Castle
A hazy black pig is seen in the castle grounds. It is thought to be the ghost of 'Hanging' Judge Jeffries, who presided at trials after the 1685 Monmouth Rebellion. The gypsy relative of one of the executed cursed Jeffries, whose ghost now takes the shape of a pig.

Piazza Terracina, the River Exe
This pleasant area becomes spooky on January nights when splashing and screams are heard in the nearby River Exe. There is never anyone there, but water is agitated. It is thought that the ghost of John Taylor, who drowned in January 1912, is re-enacting his own death.

Exeter Under Attack

William the Conqueror besieges the city

After King Harold's defeat at the Battle of Hastings in 1066, his mother Gytha led a campaign against William, who had taken the throne of England. Gytha lived in Exeter and the town was loyal to her cause. In 1068 William besieged the city and defeated Gytha. William then built Rougemont Castle in 1068.

The Civil War (1642–1649)

During the Civil War, Exeter initially supported the Parliamentarians because senior officials in the city had Parliamentarian sympathies. In 1643 the Royalists seized Exeter. Counter attacks by Parliamentarians ensued. In 1646 the citizens had had enough and surrendered. Exeter suffered terribly. Disease had spread in the enclosed city and bombardment had destroyed large areas.

The Exeter Blitz

Exeter was one of five English cities to fall victim to the Baedeker Air Raids in 1942. The *Baedeker Tourist Guide to Britain*, published in Germany, was used to select cities of historical importance to be attacked in retaliation for Allied raids on Germany. Exeter suffered several air raids, the worst being on 4 May 1942. Over 250 people were killed and several hundred more were injured. Large areas of the historic city centre were destroyed along with numerous shops and homes.

Gruesome Exeter

In January 1820 Queen Victoria's father, Edward Duke of Kent, died of pneumonia while visiting Sidmouth. The long journey back to London took several days in bad weather and the body needed to be preserved. For some reason, the family chose not to use the services of a local mortician. Instead, Edward's already pungent body was taken to the Royal Clarence Hotel in Exeter to await embalming.

Cathedral Green was a graveyard for hundreds of years. After several plague epidemics killed thousands, bodies were stacked several deep in the ground near the cathedral. In the 1630s, Bishop Hall complained of seeing bits of decaying skeleton sticking out. The protruding bones were removed to a nearby charnel house. To this day tiny fragments of bone lurk below the surface of the attractive green.

Opened in 1837, the catacombs at St Bartholomew's Cemetery were supposed to ease the problem of overcrowded graveyards. The catacombs are huge, but only around eleven internments ever took place there. Being buried in the catacombs was too expensive for most people. Today the catacombs are a creepy oddity, popular with tourists.

Festivals

Animated Exeter – February
Local and national animated film events, including workshops for all abilities. Hosted at various venues around the city.

Vibraphonic – March
A three-day music event featuring jazz, reggae, blues, soul, hip hop, dance and much more.

Exeter Food Festival – April
The largest Food Festival in the South West. Local food and drink, cooking classes, and demonstrations by top chefs, culminate in the After Dark Party in the picturesque Northernhay Garden.

Exeter Respect Festival – June
Exeter Respect promotes cultural harmony and says no to racism through music, drama and dance. There are events suitable for all ages.

Ignite: Exeter Fringe Festival – June/July
A fourteen-day live performance event in a number of locations around the city. Ignite gives a diverse range of performers the chance to showcase work in theatre, dance and comedy.

Exeter Craft Festival – July
Atmospheric Cathedral Green hosts a multitude of craft demonstrations and exhibitions featuring art, pottery, jewellery and other high-quality handmade goods.

Famous Musicians

A member of the internationally famous rock group Coldplay, **Chris Martin** was born in Exeter in 1977. He attended Exeter Cathedral School, where his musical ability soon became apparent. His parents still live near the city and Chris and his wife, Gwyneth Paltrow, visit frequently. In 1968 his grandfather, John Belsey Martin, became Mayor of Exeter. Chris is an outspoken exponent of fair trade and has visited and campaigned for farmers in many parts of the world.

Born in 1987, multi-award winning, multi-platinum soul singer and song writer **Joss Stone** grew up in Devon. Her personal fortune is estimated at £12 million, not bad for a twenty-five year old! Joss' mother, Wendy, opened the music venue Mama Stone's in Exeter in 2009. Described as 'the coolest vibe in town', Mama Stone's promotes up and coming singers and musicians. Joss herself has played sell-out gigs at the venue.

Famous Writers

Though he later became Britain's greatest Victorian novelist, in the 1830s **Charles Dickens** worked as a journalist in Exeter. In 1839 he rented Mile End Cottage in the Alphington area of Exeter for his parents; he often stayed there for peace and quiet as his fame as a writer grew. It is said that a number of Dickens' characters were based on the regulars at Exeter's Turks Head – an inn that he especially liked.

Internationally famous writer **J.R.R. Tolkien** was greatly impressed by *The Exeter Book*, a tenth-century collection of Anglo-Saxon poetry – one of the most important in the world. The speech made by Tolkien's character King Théoden in *Lord of the Rings* was inspired by the poem 'The Wanderer' from *The Exeter Book*, which is kept in the Cathedral Library.

Famous Servicemen

A lifelong soldier, **General Sir Redvers Henry Buller VC** (1839–1908) lived just outside Exeter. He served with distinction in numerous wars from the 1860s to the 1890s. In 1899, with age catching up with him, Buller was persuaded against his will to be officer in command of the Boer War. Initial campaigns were beset by failure and Buller was criticised. He remained very popular with men who had served under him. His funeral in 1908 was attended by thousands.

The Reverend Theodore Bailey Hardy VC MC DSO (1863–1918) was over fifty when the First World War broke out. Bailey Hardy left his native Exeter to volunteer as an army chaplain. His gallant actions rescuing wounded soldiers while under heavy fire soon saw him become the most decorated non-combatant of the war. In 1918 Bailey Hardy died of wounds.

Famous Sports Personalities

Born in Exeter in 1985, **Liam Tancock** is a record-breaking swimmer who specialises in the backstroke. He was a member of Exeter Swimming Club and it was there that his ambitions were stirred. In 2011 Liam won the gold medal at the World Aquatics Championships and qualified for the British Swimming Squad at the London 2012 Olympics. He is the current World Record holder in the 50m backstroke.

A member of Exeter Harriers Athletics Club for over twenty years, **Jo Pavey** is a medal-winning runner, competing primarily in 5,000m and 10,000m races. She has been the British women's champion over 5,000m five times and won a silver medal at the 2012 European Championships. More recently Jo has been having success as a marathon runner.

Other Famous People Associated with Exeter

Award-winning chef **Michael Caines** was born in Exeter in 1969. After attending Exeter Catering College, Michael worked in a number of prestigious restaurants. He was awarded an MBE in 2006 and won AA Chef of the Year in 2007. In 2000 he and a partner bought the Royal Clarence Hotel on Cathedral Green and developed the ABode Hotel chain. He is in charge of food at all these establishments. Caines' restaurant at the ABode Royal Clarence is one of the city's finest dining experiences.

Multi-talented **Baroness Floella Benjamin** is an actor, television presenter and writer. She is Vice President of Barnardos and has interests in several other charities. She was awarded an OBE for services to broadcasting in 2001 and became Chancellor of the University of Exeter in 2006.

Exeter City Football Club

History:

1904 – Club founded

1908 – Beat Weymouth 14–0

1914 – Toured South America playing several local sides

1920 – Joined the Football League

1931 – Reached 6th round of the FA Cup

1981 – Repeat of 1931 achievement

1996 – Avoided threatened closure

2008 – Promoted from the Conference League to League Two

Nickname:

The Grecians – there are many stories about the origin of this name. The oddest is that it derives from a group of poor children who used to live near the club and were called the 'Greasy 'Uns'!

Claim to fame:

Exeter City were Brazil's first ever opponents in 1914. Brazil won 2–0.

Grecians who played for England:

Dick Pym, 1925–1926

Cliff Bastin, 1930s

Lee Sharp, 1989–1995

Famous Fans:

Uri Gellar – a former club director

Chris Martin of Coldplay

The late Michael Jackson

Exeter Chiefs Rugby Club

History:
1882 – Club founded

1905 – Played against the New Zealand All Blacks

2002–2008 – Four times runner-up in the EDF Energy Trophy

2010 – Promoted to Aviva Premiership

2012 – Appeared in the Heineken Cup for the first time.

Nickname:

The Chiefs' badge features a Native American chief. Fans chant the stirring 'Tomahawks Chop', often to the sound of drums.

Chiefs who played for England:
Thomas Kelly (England Captain), 1906–1908

Tom Johnson, 2012

(Many of the Chiefs' squad play for a number of other countries)

Other Honours:
In 2012 Exeter Chiefs' chairman, Tony Rowe, was awarded an OBE in the Queen's honours list for his services to sport, charity and business.

Visiting Monarchs

932 – King Athelstan
Visited Exeter after putting down a Cornish rebellion.
Fearing further unrest, he made extensive improvements to
the city wall.

1050 – King Edward the Confessor
With his wife Queen Edith, King Edward attended the
enthronement of his friend and assistant Leofric as the first
Bishop of Exeter.

1497 – King Henry VII
Awarded Exeter his sword and Cap of Maintenance for
loyalty to him during the rebellion of Perkin Warbeck,
pretender to the throne. The sword and cap are still used in
civic processions.

Other visiting Monarchs
49 – Arviragus; 876 – Alfred; 1001 – Ethelred; 1068 – William
I; 1137 – Stephen; 1285 – Edward I; 1451 – Henry VI; 1470
– Edward IV; 1483 – Richard III; 1644 – Charles I; 1670 –
Charles II; William III

From John Gidley's *A History of Royal Visits to the Ancient and Loyal City
from AD 49 to 1863* (1863)

EDWARD the CONFESSOR

1789 – King George III

Visited Exeter with his family that August. Large crowds jostled for the best positions to view the Royal Family and several fights broke out. Railings were used for crowd control – an early example of kettling!

1915 – King George V

Came to Exeter with his wife Queen Mary during the First World War, to boost morale.

Queen Elizabeth II

Our present Queen has visited Exeter on at least five occasions – more than any other monarch. Her latest visit was in 2012, as part of her Diamond Jubilee tour of the South West. Whilst in the city, the Queen visited the Princesshay shopping centre and Exeter University, where she opened the Forum Development – a new high-tech learning facility.

Theatre

Barnfield Theatre
The venue opened in 1891 but was taken over by the Post Office after that organisation was bombed in 1942. In the 1960s, the Barnfield was used by the Inland Revenue, reopening as a theatre in 1972. It is home to Exeter's Little Theatre Co. but presents a wide range of comedy, music and drama. The 'M' Café Bar is named after 'Murphy', a long-dead volunteer who is said to haunt the building.

The Bike Shed Theatre & Bar
Opened in 2010 in a disused cellar of the bicycle business above, The Bikeshed Theatre & Bar has gone from strength to strength. It is Exeter's electrifying alternative theatre and music venue.

New Theatre
The New Theatre has been a drama school since 1979 and is home to the Cygnet Theatre Co. Public performances began in 1993. Since then the theatre has become an important part of Exeter's art scene, fulfilling the hopes of its enthusiastic directors, teachers, staff and students with innovative performances by Cygnet and other companies. The theatre is particularly encouraging of new stage writers, including the author of this book!

Northcott Theatre
The Northcott opened in 1967 as a replacement for the Theatre Royal. The playwright Harold Pinter has described the Northcott as 'beautiful'. The theatre produces high-quality professional entertainment.

114 **Then & Now**

Some Historic City Centre Pubs

The Ship Inn, St Martin's Lane
This building dates from the sixteenth century and was
reputedly the favourite inn of Sir Francis Drake. Adventurer
Sir Walter Raleigh was also a frequent visitor. In the
Victorian era the handicapped son of a landlord was accused
of murdering prostitutes here, but the accusation was never
proved. Today the Ship is known for its inexpensive, but very
good food.

The Well House Tavern, Cathedral Yard
Impressively sited opposite the cathedral, the fifteenth-
century Well House has been used by a number of businesses,
including a tailor, and a bookshop. In the basement is a well
dating from the Norman period and a glass case displaying
a mysterious skeleton. It is mixture of both male and female
bones, possibly dating from the ninth century. The pub is a
favourite of city centre workers at the end of the day.

The White Hart Inn, South Street
A former coaching inn, the atmospheric White Hart Inn was
built in the fourteenth century. The building is reputed to be
haunted – particularly on the upper floor, where a fire in the
1800s killed many people. Famous guests include the Monty
Python team, who stayed there while filming in the 1970s.
Today the inn is popular for its characterful olde world charm
and excellent food.

City developments

In November 2010 it was announced that department store John Lewis was taking over the former Debenhams building at the top of High Street. A space-age façade of curved glass houses technical innovations, including a 'computerised magic mirror' to help customers when trying on clothes. The store opened in October 2012.

In 2012, Devon County Council started examining plans for a link road between Exhibition Way and Harrington Lane. The new route, which could cost around £1 million to complete, will consist of a single carriageway and pedestrian footpath across part of Eastern Fields. It is hoped that the scheme will ease traffic problems in the Pinhoe area. Opposition from local residents – one even wrote a protest song – has been to no avail.

Exeter's City Wall – Fascinating Facts

The wall was built between AD 160 and 200.

It replaced an earth and wooden wall which was built after AD 55.

The wall is almost 2 miles long and circles the central area of the city, where the Roman's built their settlement.

Today Exeter has grown far beyond the Roman walls, as you can see from old maps.

Amazingly, 70 per cent of the wall still remains.

The Roman parts are easy to spot – they are the neatest bits! All the Roman sections have stone blocks of the same size.

The Romans used purple volcanic trap to build the wall.

Later alterations and additions were constructed using red, pink or white sandstone.

The wall was built with four main defensive gates. These were rebuilt at various times before sadly being demolished in the eighteenth century to make way for roads.

The gates were used to hang the bodies of traitors during Exeter's many conflicts.

Stocks were sited near the gates so that small-time criminals could be ridiculed by passing locals.

The gates were sometimes used for a more cheerful reason. They became unofficial drinking dens – a great way for poorly paid gatekeepers to boost their incomes!

In 1814, the wrought-iron Burnet Patch Bridge was built over a gap in the wall. This allowed the infirm mayor of the same name to inspect the wall easily. The bridge can still be seen.

You can see the wall on a free Red Coat guided tour, or by following the self-guided City Wall trail.

Exeter

122 **Iconic Image**

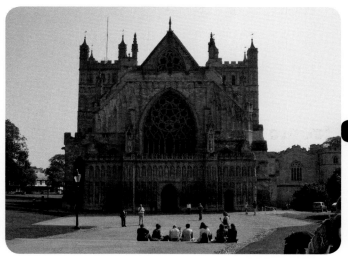

Things to do in Exeter – Checklist

Explore the quay and pick up some unusual bargains in the antique shops and craft workshops. ☐

Relax with alfresco afternoon tea outside the Royal Clarence Hotel overlooking the beautiful cathedral. ☐

Follow the informative Roman City Wall trail to learn about Exeter's Roman history. ☐

Enjoy browsing in atmospheric Gandy Street's unusual independent shops. ☐

Visit Exeter's Underground Passages for some subterranean history, and if you are feeling adventurous try the 'Crawling Passage'! ☐

Take a cruise boat from Topsham down the River Exe and along the coast for some stunning views. ☐

View the interior of the cathedral and crane your neck to see its ceiling – it boasts the longest continuous Medieval Gothic vaulting in the world. ☐

Join one of the city's Red Coat Guided Tours and learn about Exeter's fascinating history from a knowledgeable and enthusiastic guide. ☐

Watch Exeter Football Club, known locally as 'The Grecians', at their St James Park ground. ☐

Spend an afternoon at the newly extended Royal Albert Memorial Museum & Art Gallery for some great exhibits and hands on fun. ☐

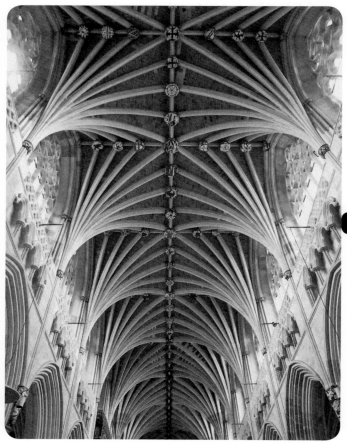

Picture Credits

All images are copyright of the author unless otherwise stated.

Page:
P.23
Rennes Port, France. (Courtesy of Exeter Council)

P.23
Bad Homburg, Germany. (Courtesy of Exeter Council)

P.25
Exeter, Ontario, Canada. (Courtesy of Bobak Ha' Eri)

P.25
Exeter, Tulare County, USA. (Courtesy of Bobak Ha' Eri)

P.26
Iron Age Settlement. (Courtesy of Exeter City Council)

P.33
Exeter Redcoat Guides. (Courtesy of Exeter City Council)

P.39
Shapter's Report on Exeter. (Courtesy of Devon and Exeter Institution)

P.41
Revd Sabine Baring Gould. (Courtesy of Devon and Exeter Institution)

P.43
Uri Gellar. (Courtesy of D. Rozhov)

P.45
Princess Henrietta Anne. (Courtesy of Exeter City Council)

P.45
Sir Francis Drake. (Courtesy of Devon and Exeter Institution)

P.49
Roman Antefix. (Courtesy of Exeter City Council)

P.53
Bishop of Exeter & Occupy Exeter. (Courtesy of David Cornforth)

P.57
Old Princesshay Shopping Centre. (Courtesy of David Cornforth)

P.65
Exeter Half Penny, 1792. (Courtesy of A. Ellis)

P.77
Drawing of Old Broadgate. (Courtesy of Richard Parker)

P.79
The Houses of Parliament. (Courtesy of Arpingstone)

P.81
Isambard Kingdom Brunel. (Courtesy of Devon and Exeter Institution)

P.83
Phil King, Mace Sergeant. (Courtesy of Exeter City Council)

P.89
Exeter Blitz. (Courtesy of David Cornforth)

P.97
Charles Dickens. (Courtesy of Devon and Exeter Institution)

P.99
General Sir Redvers Buller. (Courtesy of Devon and Exeter Institution)

P.101
Running track. (Courtesy of The History Press)

P.109
King Edward the Confessor. (Courtesy of The History Press)

P.109
King Ethelred. (Courtesy of The History Press)

P.111
George III. (Courtesy of The History Press)

P.111
George V. (Courtesy of The History Press)

P.115
Then- Exeter High Street. (Courtesy of David Cornforth)

P.125
Cathedral Ceiling. (Courtesy of the Dean and Chapter, Exeter Cathedral)